THE GOLDEN YEARS

1974

D0237069

text: David Sandison, Michael Heatley, Lorna Milne, Ian Welch

design: Paul Kurzeja

SIENA

197

Welcome to *The Golden Years* and the hurly-burly 1974, a year of events often so dramatic and far reaching, they continue to echo even today.

Richard Milhous Nixon finally paid the price of his complicity in the Watergate break-in and cover-up by becoming the first US President to resign rather than face the ultimate sanction of impeachment by a people outraged by what they'd learned. Many of his lieutenants would not get off that easily.

The unimaginable happened in London one night when shots rang out and a man tried to kidnap Princess Anne. In San Francisco, there were no shots, but heiress Patty Hearst was grabbed by a terrorist gang to begin a twisting, turning saga a Hollywood executive would reject as too fanciful if someone wrote it as a movie script.

Chrissie Evert and Jimmy Connors fell in love. The French electorate fell for the aristocratic charms of Valery Giscard d'Estaing and voted him their new President. The British decided that they preferred the promises of Harold Wilson to the reality of Edward Heath's ailing Conservative government, and put Wilson into 10 Downing Street.

Two Dukes made headlines, though for very different reasons. The death of jazz giant Duke

Ellington brought tributes from all over the world. The flight of Lord Lucan, who killed his children's nanny before vanishing, brought news of sightings from Sydney to Sweden.

Scientists proved it was possible to divide the genetic 'building block' DNA, offering new drugs, new treatments for heridatry diseases, and enhanced plant and animal breeding. Other scientists warned us, for the first time, that our industrialized society was damaging the world's ozone layer.

Glenda Jackson won an Oscar, and Muhammad Ali regained his world heavyweight crown.

It's all here, and much more besides. Good reading!

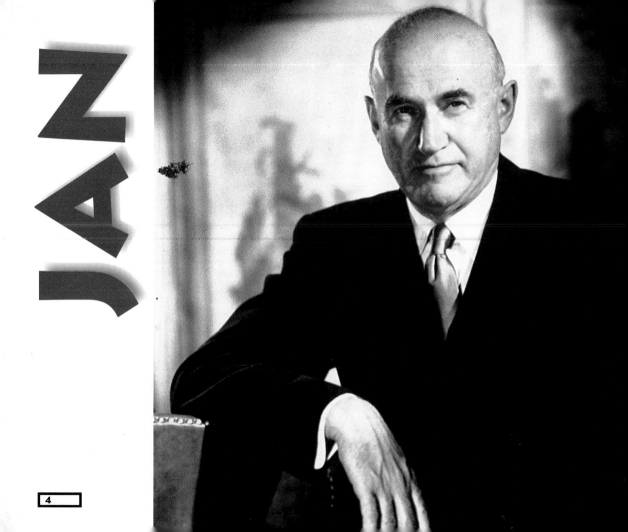

JAN

1: You Won't Find Another Fool Like Me
- The New Seekers
2: The Show Must Go On
- Leo Sayer
3: Merry Xmas Everybody
- Slade
4: My Coo-Ca-Choo
- Alvin Stardust
5: Dance With The Devil
- Cozy Powell
6: I Love You Love Me Love
- Gary Glitter
7: Forever
- Roy Wood
8: Paper Roses
- Marie Osmond
9: Radar Love
- Golden Earring
10: I Wish It Could Be Christmas Everyday
- Wizzard

JANUARY 31

End Credits For Hollywood's Sam Goldwyn

AMERICAN POPULAR ENTERTAINMENT lost one of its greatest champions today, with the death of film-producer Samuel Goldwyn in Beverly Hills. Aged 91, he had suffered a stroke.

Real name Samuel Goldfish, the Warsaw-born and raised movie mogul hit Hollywood in 1910 and quickly made a name for himself after co-producing Cecil B. DeMille's first film, *The Squaw Man,* in 1913. Going into partnership with former scrap-metal dealer Louis B. Mayer in 1924, their MGM empire became one of America's biggest and most powerful businesses.

Goldwyn's reputation as a star-maker (Danny Kaye and Eddie Cantor, to name but two) was accompanied by a refusal to make anything but family films. He quit MGM in 1942 but prospered on his own account with triumphs like *Wuthering Heights* and *Hans Christian Andersen.*

His malapropisms – like 'Include me out' and 'In two words, im-possible' – were known as Goldwynisms, but were often apocryphal. His legendary reputation was not.

JANUARY 22

Northern Ireland Assembly Collapses

Brian Faulkner's resignation as leader of the Ulster Unionist Party sparked a huge row in Stormont today when a number of extremist Protestants took exception to having to share power with Catholics on the province's Executive Council.

The mace – symbol of parliamentary authority – was seized and passed around the chamber, hard-liners spat at fellow Unionists, and the Reverend Ian Paisley had to be evicted from the chamber by police.

Faulkner would remain chief executive of the 'cabinet' now in obvious disarray, but the mood in Ulster was typified by the murders, later in the month, of two Catholic workers. They were killed by hooded gunmen as sectarian violence increased.

JANUARY 2

British Museums Charge For Admission

A total of 18 national galleries and museums throughout the UK began charging admission fees to the general public today, for the first time in their history.
Governors defended their break with a tradition which had always viewed the right to knowledge as a public service, explaining that rising costs and reduced government support-grants had forced them to act.

New Breakthrough For Barnard   JANUARY 25

Dr Christian Barnard, the South African pioneer-surgeon who carried out the world's first successful heart transplant in 1967, today made history for a second time when he carried out the first operation to transplant a heart into a patient without removing his original organ. The operation, which was aimed at supplementing the original instead of completely replacing it, was intended to provide a better answer than the make-or-break of a complete transplant.

The 52-year-old surgeon carried out the operation at the Groote Schuur Hospital, in Cape Town, the scene of his first triumph.

Nixon's Watergate Troubles Mount As Tapes Are Heard

THE MORASS OF ACCUSATION, denial, demands and refusals into which the Washington Grand Jury investigating the Watergate conspiracy had recently sunk became very murky waters for President Nixon this month when he was forced to hand over 500 tapes and papers implicated in what had become widely recognized as a major conspiracy.

On January 4, the President was served a subpoena ordering the surrender of tapes he had admitted were made of conversations he'd had with aides in the White House. He had arranged for the Oval Office to be wired for sound, he said, so an accurate archive could be built to aid him write future memoirs.

Originally refusing to hand the material over, Nixon was forced to back down. Only a week later, the court was told there were five gaps in the tapes. Some explaining would have to be done.

Tex Ritter Rides Into Last Sunset

One of America's most popular cowboy film stars in the 1930s and '40s, Tex Ritter said 'So long, pardners' for the last time today, when he died, aged 69. A highly successful recording artist - he recorded the original version of *Do Not Forsake Me Oh My Darlin'* which was featured in the Oscar-winning movie *High Noon* - he had been elected to the Country Music Hall of Fame in 1964.

Born Woodward Maurice Ritter, in Texas, he had planned a law career while attending the University of Texas, but he caught the acting bug, moved to New York and made a number of successful Broadway stage appearances before heading for Hollywood in 1936.

Signed to Grand National Pictures, Ritter began a long career as a singing cowboy star, rivalling Gene Autry and Roy Rogers at his peak. When the popularity of that genre faded, Ritter moved to Nashville to record full-time, became a prominent member of the business community and, in 1970, ran (unsuccessfully) for the US Senate.

Sunday Football Kicks Off

The first professional football match to be played in Britain on a Sunday was staged today at Millwall FC's Den ground in South London - because of a shortage of available dates.
Played against Millwall's London rivals, Fulham, it was won by a single goal to the home side but attracted 15,134 supporters to a humble Division Two game, showing the potential of moving games from the week's major shopping-day.
By the mid-1990s, many matches would be played on Sundays, often at the behest of satellite television, while the FA Cup semifinals and League (CocaCola) Cup Final had also been moved to the sabbath, despite fierce lobbying from the Lord's Day Observance Society.

FEB

Ronnie's Son Helps Him Beat Extradition

Arrested and held by Brazilian police today when Scotland Yard detectives presented paperwork to force his extradition to Britain, Great Train Robber Ronnie Biggs had a trick up his sleeve ready to deal - the young son born to him and his Brazilian girlfriend.

Under Brazilian law, Biggs - on the run since escaping from the prison term he'd been given for his part in the theft of £2.6 million ($5.2m) from a Royal Mail train in 1964 - could not, as the father of a Brazilian national, be extradited.

Ronnie knew that. His lawyers knew that. The Scotland Yard detectives left for London empty-handed.

IRA Bomb Blasts British Army Bus

THE VIOLENCE which so divided Northern Ireland crossed over to the British mainland with a vengeance again today when eleven people died in a bomb attack on a coach carrying servicemen and their families on the M62 motorway near Bradford, Yorkshire.

At least one child was among the dead, some of whom had been thrown 250 yards by the force of the explosion. A fleet of TEN ambulances was required to carry the injured to nearby hospitals.

Amid understandable public revulsion and outrage, police would arrest Judith Ward, a 'Troops Out of Ulster' activist. Charged and found guilty of planting the bomb, in November she would be sentenced to 30 years in prison.

Solzhenitsyn Expelled From Homeland

After the manuscript of his book *The Gulag Archipelago* – exposing the appalling conditions of Stalin's labour camps – fell into KGB hands, author Alexander Solzhenitsyn was forcibly taken from his flat in Moscow's Gorky Street today and put on a flight to Frankfurt, West Germany, where he was given temporary refuge by the German author, Heinrich Boll. The book, which Solzhenitsyn had concealed to protect those who appeared in it, would subsequently be published in Paris, exposing Soviet internal affairs to an embarrassing degree.

Soviet authorities later announced that Solzhenitsyn's wife – who had strenuously tried to prevent his removal from their home – and children would be permitted to join him in exile in the West. Eventually making his home in the US, Solzhenitsyn would not return to Russia until 1995.

UK TOP 10 SINGLES

1: Tiger Feet
- Mud
2: Teenage Rampage
- Sweet
3: Solitaire
- Andy Williams
4: The Man Who Sold The World
- Lulu
5: Dance With The Devil
- Cozy Powell
6: Devil Gate Drive
- Suzi Quatro
7: Rockin' Roll Baby
- The Stylistics
8: All Of My Life
- Diana Ross
9: The Show Must Go On
- Leo Sayer
10: The Wombling Song
- The Wombles

FEBRUARY 28

Heath Out, Wilson Back, As Miners' Strike Forces UK Election

The all-out miners' strike finally brought down the British Government today when Prime Minister Edward Heath called a general election, asking the British electorate to decide with their votes whether he and the Conservative Party, or Labour and the trade unions, should run the country.

Not surprisingly, the miners were unsympathetic to Heath's appeal to call off their strike for the duration of the election campaign, although the curfew he had imposed to save electricity – which had cut short each evening's TV viewing at 10.30 pm - was not lifted until after the election. The result saw Labour's Harold Wilson (pictured) back in power after initial negotiations between Edward Heath and Liberal leader Jeremy Thorpe failed to produce a working coalition. Wilson's third term of office began inauspiciously, however, with his party actually outnumbered in the Commons.

Heiress Patty Hearst Kidnapped

NINETEEN-YEAR-OLD NEWSPAPER HEIRESS Patricia (Patty) Campbell Hearst, the granddaughter of millionaire William Randolph Hearst, was abducted from her San Francisco home by members of the left-wing Symbionese Liberation Army (SLA) today. Ransom notes addressed to her father, Randolph Hearst, demanded the distribution of food to the poor of the city to ensure her safe return.

Patty would cause a sensation by appearing to sympathize with her captors' cause, although she subsequently claimed to have been brainwashed by the group. But when she took part in a bank-raid by SLA members, after which six of the robbers were killed during a shoot-out with Los Angeles police, Hearst went into hiding with those who were left.

Finally tracked down by the FBI in 1975, Patty would be tried and sentenced to seven years in prison for her part in the robbery. She would serve less than three years of that sentence when it was commuted by the personal intervention of President Jimmy Carter.

Carnage In Cambodia As Cease-Fire Fails

The rebel forces of communist leader Pol Pot shelled the Cambodian capital, Phnom Penh, today, breaking an eight-day cease-fire in the country's long and bloody civil war.

During what was the heaviest attack in two years, the half-hour barrage killed 159 people and wounded 46 more. A large part of the shanty-town neighbourhood targeted by rebel artillery was burned to the ground as wind fanned the flames.

US President Richard Nixon once again pledged his country's support to assist Cambodia's Prime Minister Lon Nol in his fight against rebels.

World Record Air Death-Toll

THE CRASH OF A TURKISH AIRLINES DC-10
near Paris, today, claimed the lives of all 344 passengers
and crew, making it the worst crash in aviation history.
The fully loaded flight, *en route* from Orly Airport, Paris,
to London, came down in the forest of Ermerville,
cutting a swath almost a mile in length before it exploded.

Several bodies and part of the fuselage were found seven
miles from the main crash site, a popular beauty-spot
frequented by Parisians and their families. That resembled
a war scene, with wreckage and bodies strewn over a
large area. The number of fatalities was nearly twice that
of the worst previous crash.

Structural failure at 10,000 feet would eventually be
blamed for the crash. Experts believed one of the DC-
10's three engines may have exploded, but evidence from
the badly damaged 'black box' flight-recorder was
inconclusive.

Reagan Enters Hearst Case Feet-First

Ronald Reagan, the Governor of
California, today entered the Patty
Hearst kidnap drama - and caused
an immediate outcry - when he
attacked the Hearst family's
decision to submit to the
kidnappers' demands to distribute
free food to the poor and homeless
of San Francisco.

This had been one of the first
principal ransom conditions
stipulated by the Symbionese
Liberation Army group who'd
kidnapped Patty last month.

Complaining about the grudging
response of some who'd received
food parcels, Governor Reagan
pronounced, 'It's just too bad we
can't have an epidemic of
botulism!' Within days, the Hearst
family received a new taped
message from Patty urging them to
do - and pay - more for her
release.

UK TOP 10 SINGLES

1: The Air That I Breathe
- The Hollies

2: Billy, Don't Be A Hero
- Paper Lace

3: Jealous Mind
- Alvin Stardust

4: You're Sixteen
- Ringo Starr

5: The Most Beautiful Girl
- Charlie Rich

6: My Happiness
- Connie Francis

7: Remember (Sha-La-La)
- The Bay City Rollers

8: Jet
- Paul McCartney & Wings

9: The Wombling Song
- The Wombles

10: It's You
- Freddie Starr

MARCH 15

Corrupt Architect Jailed

Discredited British architect John Poulson, 63, was given a seven-year prison sentence by a Leeds court today after being found guilty of bribing public officials with expensive holidays and gifts to win UK public-sector contracts.

The jury had already found Poulson - whose contacts in high places included the former Home Secretary, Reginald Maudling - guilty of seven other offences a few weeks earlier. It heard that he and his principal partner in crime, builder T. Dan Smith (who was also jailed), had handed out more than half a million pounds to local government officials.

The corruption scandal exposed the dirty dealings of more than one rotten borough. Today's sentence was to run concurrently with the five-year prison term imposed on Poulson last month.

MARCH 1

Liberal Party Enjoys Balance Of Power

The Liberal Party, along with the Scottish and Welsh National parties, found itself holding the balance of power in Britain after the February 28 general election.

Liberal leader Jeremy Thorpe was riding high as he was wooed, first by the Conservative Party's Edward Heath, and then by the new Labour Prime Minister, Harold Wilson.

The Liberals emerged from the election with 23.6 per cent of the vote – their best showing since 1935 and one that appeared to confirm them as a viable third force in British politics. Jeremy Thorpe's refusal to form a coalition with Edward Heath meant the Conservatives did not have the working majority they needed to continue in government, forcing Heath to concede victory to Harold Wilson.

MARCH 16

Stevie's A Wonder As He Collects Five Grammies

It was a busy and triumphant evening in New York for Stevie Wonder when he took the honours - and made five acceptance speeches - as his *Innervisions* album proved the most successful in the annual Grammy Awards.

Besides winning the Album of the Year award, Innervisions won trophy for being the Best Engineered Album, while it also delivered prizes for the Best Pop Vocal Performance *(You Are The Sunshine Of My Life),* the Best R & B Song and Best R & B Vocal Performance (for *Superstition*).

MARCH 20

Bullets Fly In Princess Anne Kidnap Attempt

A WOULD-BE KIDNAPPER tonight fired six shots at a car carrying Princess Anne and her husband, Captain Mark Phillips, as they travelled down The Mall near Buckingham Palace in London after an evening out. One of the bullets passed between the princess and Capt. Phillips and, while neither of them was hurt in the attack, their bodyguard, chauffeur, a policeman and a taxi driver were injured.

The gunman, Ian Ball, then tried to drag Princess Anne from the car, but fled into St James's Park when the bodyguard drew a pistol. He was later arrested by police.

When charged with attempted murder, Ball - who said he was intent on a £1 million ransom demand if he'd succeeded - claimed that he'd staged the assault to highlight Britain's lack of mental care facilities.

MARCH 10

War Is Over, Honest!

If you ever felt overwhelmed by the speed of world events and unable to keep up, spare a thought for the Japanese soldier found alive today on the tiny Philippine island of Lubang, still wearing the tattered remnants of the battle-dress he'd been issued during World War II - a conflict he was unaware had ended 29 years earlier! The lone warrior took some convincing before he surrendered and allowed himself to be flown to the mainland, where his return to the real world could begin. They don't make soldiers - or uniforms - like that any more!

Mariner Probe Scans Mercury

Mariner 10, the latest in a series of US space probes which had already provided information on the inner planets Mercury, Venus and Mars, survived a seemingly endless series of malfunctions to accomplish the first ever two-planet space mission today when it began to transmit pictures of Mercury back to Earth. During its recent encounter with Venus, *Mariner 10* had used that planet as a 'springboard' to redirect itself towards Mercury. After this first Mercury fly-by, the spacecraft would encounter the planet every time Mercury went twice around the Sun, giving *Mariner 10* three encounters with the Sun's nearest neighbour before its fuel ran out.

Today's encounter saw the probe pass only 705 km (438 miles) from the planet. It detected a weak magnetic field (unexpected by scientists for such a slowly rotating planet) and an atmosphere considerably less dense than the Earth's. Photographs showed a Moon-like surface and 'compression scarps'– cliffs formed by the wrinkling skin of a contracting planet, and unknown on Mars or the Moon.

GODFATHER II STEALS OSCARS

In the 1972 Academy Awards ceremony, Francis Ford Coppola had the unhappy experience of seeing his 11-times nominated *The Godfather* win only three Oscars. It was swamped by the Bob Fosse-directed *Cabaret's* eight awards, and while Coppola had shared the Adapted Screenplay Oscar with novelist Mario Puzo, he had lost out on the treasured Best Director award to the debutant Fosse.

This year Coppola was back, with *The Godfather, Part II.* But so was Bob Fosse, with *Lenny,* a forceful portrayal of satirical comedian Lenny Bruce, starring Dustin Hoffman. French superstar François Truffaut was also short-listed for his first US-funded movie, *Day For Night,* along with the maverick Roman Polanski, with his stylish *Chinatown,* and actor-director John Cassavetes with the arty *A Woman Under The Influence.*

By the end of the evening, Coppola could finally breathe easier. Not only had *The Godfather, Part II* repeated the Best Picture win of its predecessor, but he had finally secured possession of the gold statuette which named him Best Director. Just for good measure, he and Puzo also collected second Adapted Screenplay awards.

Although Al Pacino lost out for a second time (in 1972 he'd been nominated for a Supporting Actor, but now he was the new Don Corleone he was up for Best Actor) when Art Carney won for *Harry And Tonto* in a contest which also included Albert Finney (as Hercules Poirot in *Murder On The Orient Express*), Dustin Hoffman (*Lenny*) and Jack Nicholson (*Chinatown*).

Robert De Niro did succeed in winning the Supporting Actor award for *The Godfather, Part II,* beating Fred Astaire (nominated for his playing in the Best Picture-nominated *The Towering Inferno*), Jeff Bridges (for the very silly *Thunderbolt and Lightning*) and fellow *Godfather II* actors Lee Strasberg and Michael V Gazzo.

The Best Actress prize was justly won by Ellen Burstyn, for her outstanding performance in *Alice Doesn't Live Here Anymore.* She beat off the challenges of Faye Dunaway (*Chinatown*), Gena Rowlands (*A Woman Under The Influence*), Valerie Perrine (*Lenny*) and Diahann Carroll (*Claudine*).

Ingrid Bergman was voted Best Supporting Actress for her performance in *Murder On The Orient Express,* beating the supervamp of *Blazing Saddles* delivered by Madeline Kahn, Valentina Cortese (*For Day For Night*), Diane Ladd (*Alice Doesn't Live Here Anymore*) and Talia Shire (*The Godfather, Part II*).

The awards won by *The Towering Inferno* were, fittingly, mainly technical - cinematography and editing - though the film's theme song, *We May Never Love Like This Again,* won an Oscar for Al Kasha and Joel Hirschhorn. The year's other disaster movie (in every sense of the word), *Earthquake,* was awarded the sound and visual effects Oscars.

Generally agreed to be Stiff Of The Year, *The Great Gatsby* scraped in with one Oscar for Theoni V Aldredge's costume designs, and a second for Nelson Riddle's Adapted Score. Nino Rota and Carmine Coppola's Original Dramatic Score Oscar added to the *Godfather, Part II* tally, as did Dean Tavoularis and Angelo Graham's art direction.

But, that said, *The Godfather, Part II* was not a classic, just as 1974 had not proved a great year for films.

Al Pacino in *The Godfather, Part II*

APRIL

APRIL 20

Streaking Craze Hits Britain

STREAKING - the US craze of running naked through public places - arrived in Britain with a bang today when the first recorded streaker made an unashamed appearance during a live televised rugby match between England and France at London's Twickenham ground. The gentleman in question was escorted from the pitch by attendant policemen, one of whose helmets was strategically placed in order to maintain a degree of decorum!

Begun on American college campuses, streaking had recently emerged as an unbilled bonus at rock concerts by Yes, Gregg Allman and The Beach Boys. Famous rock promoter Bill Graham had actually done it himself, as had Beach Boys Dennis Wilson and Mike Love, much to the delight of their fans.

Not even the Oscars ceremony was safe from the exhibitionism of one Robert Opal, who disrupted proceedings with a naked dash through the event on April 3, inspiring Master of Ceremonies David Niven to quip, 'The only award that man is ever likely to get will be for stripping and showing off his shortcomings!'

Quick to recognize the hit potential of the craze, US novelty pop singer Ray Stevens recorded the wacky *The Streak,* which went on to sell more than a million copies on both sides of the Atlantic.

APRIL 1

Britain Changes Shape

In an effort to improve the efficiency of local government, virtually every county in England and Wales had its boundaries redrawn today, in the biggest reorganization since 1888.

Counties and boroughs which could trace their roots back as far as the Middle Ages simply ceased to exist at the stroke of a pen – the Yorkshire and Lincolnshire Ridings, Cumberland, Westmorland and Huntingdonshire all disappeared, while the tiny county of Rutland was swallowed up by Leicestershire.

Six new metropolitan counties were created in a move which underlined the shift from country to city-based administration.

APRIL 25

Government Falls As Portuguese Military Take Over

Portugal's right-wing government was ousted today by a military coup by young officers determined to end their country's involvement in wars in her African colonies.

The so-called Junta of Salvation immediately granted all of Portugal's colonies independence, and war hero General Spinola, the coup leader, promised an early return to democratic government. The coup, and Spinola's promise, prompted the return to Portugal of exiled socialist leader Mario Soares, polarizing left and right-wing politics in the country.

Bank Cameras Catch Patty Hearst In Robbery

Suspicions that kidnapped publishing empire heiress Patty Hearst had been persuaded to join the struggle of her Symbionese Liberation Army (SLA) captors appeared to be confirmed today when the 19-year-old was captured by security cameras in a San Francisco bank, wearing a wig and waving a machine-gun.

This stunning development, which made Hearst an immediate quarry for FBI detectives attempting to track down the SLA, followed the release of a statement which revealed that she had taken the name 'Tania'. Kidnap experts said it was not unusual for hostage victims to 'bond' with their abductors.

Finally caught and sentenced to seven years in prison after her defence - that she'd been coerced into her much-publicized actions - was rejected by a California jury, Patty Hearst would have her sentence commuted by President Jimmy Carter in 1979, and would marry the detective assigned to protect her.

UK TOP 10 SINGLES

1: Seasons In The Sun
- Terry Jacks
2: Angel Face
- The Glitter Band
3: Everyday
- Slade
4: Remember Me This Way
- Gary Glitter
5: You Are Everything
- Diana Ross
6: Billy, Don't Be A Hero
- Paper Lace
7: Emma
- Hot Chocolate
8: The Cat Crept In
- Mud
9: Doctor's Orders
- Sunny
10: Seven Seas Of Rhye
- Queen

APRIL 2

President Pompidou Dies

GEORGES POMPIDOU, the President of France who had been seriously ill for some time, died today at his official residence, the Elysée Palace, in Paris. He was 63.

A former literature teacher, Pompidou was director of President Charles de Gaulle's cabinet between 1958 and 1959, becoming Prime Minister in 1962. Disputes with de Gaulle led to his dismissal in 1968, but he succeeded the general as President after the latter's death a year later.

Pompidou's death would mark a gradual movement away from insular Gaullist policies in favour of the wider interests of the Common Market (European Union). Despite his illness, Pompidou had continued to carry out official duties with brave good humour, and once commented famously to American Secretary of State Henry Kissinger, 'Every time someone shakes my hand, I think they're trying to take my pulse!'

APRIL 5

Richard Crossman, Labour Diarist, Dies

Britain's Labour Party lost one of its most distinguished, articulate and astute personalities today, with the death of Richard Crossman. He was 67.

A former Oxford don and editor of the influential *New Statesman* magazine, Crossman did not enter a political life in Parliament until 1945.

Election campaign manager for Hugh Gaitskell, Crossman joined Harold Wilson's first cabinet as Minister of Housing in 1964.

Awarded a life peerage shortly before his death, Crossman continued to make waves after his death when the detailed and frank diaries of his political life were published to cast a fresh light on the true workings of government.

APRIL 10

Israel's Golda Meir Quits

Golda Meir, Israel's long-serving and formidable Prime Minister, resigned from her post today, the victim of bitter rows which had split both her Labour Party cabinet and Israeli public opinion. The cause of the conflict was alleged deficiencies in military planning during last October's Yom Kippur War, during which Israel suffered its first setback at the hands of the Arabs.

The Labour Party was split three ways, with the majority blaming Defence Minister Moshe Dayan for failing to secure strategic territory on the East Bank of the Jordan. Despite being vindicated by an official report, Dayan was still under pressure to resign.

Rather than bow to opposition pressure to sack Dayan, Golda Meir decided that she would go instead.

APRIL 6

Abba Score Eurovision Win With 'Waterloo'

Destined to become one of the world's biggest-selling pop acts in the second half of the 1970s, Swedish pop group Abba made their international mark tonight in Brighton when they won the Eurovision Song Contest with their song *Waterloo*.
The quartet - Benny Andersson, Björn Ulvaeus, his wife Agnetha Falstög and Norwegian-born Anni-Frid Lynstad - would enjoy staggering success with Waterloo. Written by Andersson, Ulvaeus and their manager, Stig Andersson, it would top the charts in Britain, Sweden, Norway, Denmark, Holland, Belgium and Luxembourg, and reach No. 6 in the US, selling more than five million copies in the process.

MAY 28

Ulster Leaders Toppled By Strikes

A seven-day general strike called and organized by militant Ulster Unionists succeeded in forcing Prime Minister Brian Faulkner, and the members of his power-sharing executive, to resign today. The crisis effectively ended all hopes of the province having a government or administration of its own, and Ulster would begin to be governed directly from Westminster.

Food and fuel shortages, power cuts, and unofficial street barricades brought the province to a standstill. Calls from Faulkner and other more moderate leaders, and a 'back to work' march by official trade unions, failed to change workers' minds. Although there were claims that some wavering strikers had been threatened by paramilitary forces, the British Government did not use troops to break the strike.

MAY 18

India Tests First A-Bomb

The desert in Rajasthan was rocked today by the underground explosion of India's first nuclear bomb, which created a crater measuring 26 acres in area.

The test raised alarm in the world's political community, especially in Pakistan, India's closest neighbour and long-time enemy, where the possibility of an Indian nuclear attack was voiced as a potent fear. Although the 1963 Test-Ban Treaty, of which India was a signatory, forbade nuclear tests in the air or on land, underground testing was permitted. While Indian Prime Minister Indira Gandhi emphasized the 'peaceful' potential of nuclear power, her vastly expensive nuclear programme faced severe criticism within a country where more than 200 million still lived in poverty.

Willy Brandt Quits As Spy Scandal Hits Germany

WEST GERMAN CHANCELLOR Willy Brandt was forced to resign his five-year reign after the revelation that one of his most trusted aides, Gunter Guillaume, had been working as an East German spy for the past four years.

Combined with the revelation that Brandt had ignored intelligence service warnings of Guillaume's suspected allegiance, the disclosure was too severe a blow for Brandt's career to survive. He had consistently worked for better relations with East Germany, and the presence of a spy in his closest circles made him appear a gullible dupe.

Born in Lübeck in 1913, Brandt's early socialist beliefs put him in direct conflict with the emergent Nazi Party. He fled to Norway in 1933 and changed his real name (Karl Herbert Frahm) to Willy Brandt to confuse Hitler's secret police. An active member of the German and Norwegian Resistance movements during WWII, he returned to West Germany in 1945, serving as West Berlin's mayor from 1957 to 1966.

Despite his resignation, Brandt would remain active in politics, serving as chairman of the Socialist International, a worldwide confederation of socialist democratic parties, and heading the Independent Commission on International Development Issues.

Former Defence Minister Helmut Schmidt was to succeed Brandt as Chancellor, a post he would hold for the next eight years. Whereas Brandt had worked hard to improve West Germany's ties with the Eastern Bloc, Schmidt turned his sights more firmly towards the West.

UK TOP 10 SINGLES

1: Waterloo
- Abba

2: Don't Stay Away Too Long
- Peters & Lee

3: Shang-A-Lang
- The Bay City Rollers

4: Sugar Baby Love
- The Rubettes

5: Remember You're A Womble
- The Wombles

6: Rock 'n' Roll Winter
- Wizzard

7: Homely Girl
- The Chi-Lites

8: The Night Chicago Died
- Paper Lace

9: A Walkin' Miracle
- Limmie & The Family Cookin'

10: Red Dress
- Alvin Stardust

MAY 24

Jazz World Mourns Duke Ellington

Band-leader, pianist and composer Duke Ellington - born Edward Kennedy Ellington in the final year of the last century - took his final bow today after a long fight against lung cancer. This quintessential jazzman and composer of over 6,000 numbers was one of the most influential figures in the history of the music. Renowned for such classics as *Mood Indigo, Sophisticated Lady, Take The A Train, Satin Doll* and *Solitude,* his band established itself in the late 1920s and early 1930s with an initial residency at New York's legendary Cotton Club.

 Some band-members stayed with Ellington for 30 years, and the low turnover in personnel enabled individual band-members – such as saxophonists Johnny Hodges and Harry Carney, clarinettist Barney Bigard, trumpeter Cootie Williams and trombonists Lawrence Brown and Juan Tizol – to experiment widely with the form and style created by Ellington and his long-time collaborator, arranger Billy Strayhorn.

Invited by President Nixon to celebrate his seventieth birthday in the White House, where Ellington's father had once been a butler, the Duke sent Christmas cards to close friends early this month. Aware that he wouldn't be around to celebrate another, it was his unique way of saying farewell.

Giscard Is New French President

IN FRANCE TODAY, Independent Republican Valéry Giscard d'Estaing narrowly won the race for the French Presidency, overhauling socialist François Mitterrand who'd won the first round of the two-leg national leadership challenge.

In the final count, Giscard d'Estaing - at 48 the youngest French Head of State since Louis Napoleon in 1848 - claimed 50.8 per cent of the vote to Mitterrand's 49.2 per cent.

The new President first entered the National Assembly in 1956, rising quickly to become the late President Pompidou's Minister of Finance in 1962. Despite basing his campaign on reforms which included a rise in the basic wage, Giscard d'Estaing still faced French trade union threats of widespread strikes. However, he would be able to ride out that storm, and was to remain in office until 1981.

Freedom For Timothy As Turks Relent

Timothy Davey, the 17-year-old British youngster jailed three years ago in Turkey after being found guilty of trying to smuggle cannabis out of the country, was finally allowed to walk free today after an international campaign to secure his release finally proved too embarrassing for the Turkish Government.

Timothy's story would form the basis of the hugely successful Alan Parker film *Midnight Express,* which was scripted by Oliver Stone, who would win an Academy Award for his contribution.

US Contraceptive Controversy

The infamous IUD (intra-uterine device) contraceptive, developed and marketed by the US company, A.H. Robbins, made history as much for the lawsuits which resulted from its use, as it did for the misery and discomfort suffered by women who had been fitted with it. After just three years on the market, the US Food and Drug Administration today forced Robbins to withdraw its 'Dalkon Shield' after five million had been sold worldwide.

So effective was Robbins' marketing that nearly half of all IUD users were fitted with the shield, which carried a 10 per cent pregnancy risk rate compared with only 3 per cent for other devices. It was found to cause severe infections, miscarriage, infertility, chronic pain and even death.

Robbins challenged the thousands of lawsuits that were brought, but eventually faced bankruptcy. A trust fund for victims was set up with what remained of the company's assets.

JUNE

Flixborough Fire-Ball Razes Village

TWENTY-NINE PEOPLE were killed today when a massive explosion ripped through a chemical plant at Flixborough on Humberside, devastating the tiny village of just 200 inhabitants for which the factory represented a sole source of employment.

The force of the blast was such that people in Scunthorpe, four miles away, were thrown to the ground. A hundred houses in Flixborough were razed to the ground and an emergency mass evacuation of injured and stunned villagers began as a pall of toxic smoke spread over the surrounding countryside.

A build-up of steam and fumes was said to have caused the explosion. Although an alarm siren was sounded, the central control rooms of the plant became a mass of flame and molten metal only seconds later. All the dead were working in that area of the plant. As an official inquiry was set up to investigate the disaster, a number of calls were made for chemical plants never to be built near residential communities.

Prince Charles Speaks!

Prince Charles, the 25-year-old heir to the British throne, made his maiden speech to a crowded House of Lords today. He was the first future king to do so for almost 90 years.

Nixon At Soviet Summit

Despite gaining a well-deserved reputation as a rabid anti-communist in the late 1940s and early '50s while he was a legal adviser to Senator Joe McCarthy and other members of the notorious House Committee for UnAmerican Activities, President Richard Nixon emerged as a strong peacemaker during what would prove his last international tour.

That was exemplified today when he and Soviet premier Leonid Brezhnev greeted each other warmly during the third superpower summit in Moscow, prior to continuing to make positive progress in arms reduction talks.

Always strong on foreign affairs, it was perhaps appropriate that Nixon's last months in office were also spent brokering peace in the Middle East, and included the signing of a trade agreement with Egyptian President Anwar Sadat.

UK TOP 10 SINGLES

1: Hey Rock And Roll
- Showaddywaddy

2: There's A Ghost In My House
- R Dean Taylor

3: The Streak
- Ray Stevens

4: This Town Ain't Big Enough For The Both Of Us
- Sparks

5: Sugar Baby Love
- The Rubettes

6: Judy Teen
- Cockney Rebel

7: Always Yours
- Gary Glitter

8: Jarrow Song
- Alan Price

9: The Night Chicago Died
- Paper Lace

10: A Touch Too Much
- Arrows

Russia Mourns Zhukov, Saviour Of Moscow

The tears shed in Russia today on the death of Marshal Georgi Zhukov, one of the Soviet Union's most distinguished military strategists, were not the crocodile tears so common when old warhorses die. Aged 77, he was a genuine folk hero.

Conscripted into the Tsar's army as a boy,

Zhukov joined the Red Army after the Russian Revolution and became an expert in armoured warfare. As Stalin's Chief of Staff in WWII, he lifted the German siege of Moscow, masterminded the counter-offensive to recapture Stalingrad, and led the campaigns to capture both Warsaw and Berlin.

It was Zhukov who accepted the German surrender on behalf of the Soviet High Command in May 1945, and he later became Soviet Minister of Defence. Dismissed and disgraced by Khrushchev when he succeeded Stalin as Soviet leader, Zhukov may have died in obscurity, but he did not die unmourned.

DEPARTURES

Died this month:
10: Prince Henry William Frederick Albert, Duke of Gloucester, aged 74
18: Marshal Georgi Zhukov, Soviet World War II hero *(see main story)*
24: Darius Milhaud, French composer, aged 82

JUNE 17

IRA Bomb Westminster Palace

The IRA struck at the very heart of British history and tradition today - and scored an unprecedented propaganda coup - when it exploded a 20-pound bomb at the Palace of Westminster in London.

Westminster Hall, which had withstood the toll of time for almost 877 years and had presided over the lying in state of Britain's monarchs, was severely damaged as the initial explosion gave way to a series of random fires which left 11 people injured.

Police believed that the construction of a new underground car park for the House of Commons could have given the bombers a chance to pose as project workmen to gain access.

As an investigation began, press and TV pundits suggested that if the IRA could circumvent the palace's strict security so easily, nowhere in Britain could be considered safe.

JUNE 4

Amin Death-Toll Announced

There was grim news today from the International Committee of Jurists, the independent organization dedicated to investigating alleged cases of the misuse of power on a worldwide basis.

A report on the worsening situation in Uganda revealed that as many as 250,000 people had been killed in the African State since President Idi Amin overthrew President Milton Obote and came to power in January 1971.

JUNE 20

Swedish Superstar Borg Wins French Open

Aged only 18, Swedish tennis ace Björn Borg became the youngest ever winner of the French Open today, beating Manuel Orantes in five sets.

The apparently unflappable youngster, whose long hair and headband would become a familiar sight in the decade to come, would go on to win the French Open a further five times, also winning the Wimbledon singles title in five consecutive years from 1976.

Bolshoi's Baryshnikov In Shock Defection

IN THE MOST DRAMATIC EPISODE of its kind since 1961, when Russian ballet star Rudolph Nureyev escaped from KGB 'minders' to gain political asylum in Paris, 26-year-old Mikhail Baryshnikov - renowned for his sensational turns and leaps, and described by many as 'the new Nureyev' - became the latest Soviet dancer to defect to the West today.

Following an official reception in Toronto, Canada, Baryshnikov eluded KGB men and, helped by Canadian police officers, made a break for a waiting car. He was on tour with the famous Bolshoi Ballet, whose performances in London three weeks earlier had been the subject of a demonstration by friends of Kirov Ballet stars Valery Panov and his wife, who'd been refused permission to leave the Soviet Union.

Citing artistic restraints and the narrowness of the Bolshoi's repertoire as his reasons for wishing to leave, Baryshnikov would go on to work with the American Ballet Theatre and the New York City Ballet, both as dancer and director, as well as appearing as an actor in a number of films.

JUNE

WORLD CUP: 'KAISER' FRANZ SWEEPS AWAY CRUYFF'S 'TOTAL FOOTBALL'

There were two main questions being asked as this year's World Cup tournament began in West Germany, 'would the South American teams fare any better in Europe than they had in the past?' - which was not very well - and 'would the so-called 'total football' of Holland and Poland – a break from rigid formation which introduced the concept of rotation play - prove capable of defeating the more strictly disciplined teams, most especially the host nation?'

The answer to the first was a conditional negative, because although Brazil - now without the wondrous Pele, who was enjoying his first retirement - did well enough to reach the third-place game (which they lost 0-1 to Poland), neither Chile nor Uruguay survived the opening group games, and Argentina finished bottom of their group in the second round, losing two of three and managing only a single point from their 1-1 draw with East Germany.

The second question hung tantalizingly in the air until the final stages because, while Holland emerged winners of their first-round group with solid wins over Uruguay (2-0) and Bulgaria (4-1), they could only draw 1-1 with Sweden, a strictly-formationed side which was clearly modelled on the West German ideal.

For their part, Poland had sailed through their opening group, beating Argentina 3-2, World Cup débutants Haiti 7-1 and 1970 finalists Italy 2-1. In the second round they had the misfortune to be drawn in the same group as West Germany (who beat them 1-0) and had to be content with that third-place play-off against Brazil as the hosts also beat Yugoslavia 2-0 and Sweden 4-2 to win their place in the final in the Olympic Stadium in Munich.

Holland, likewise, had won all their second round games (Argentina 4-1, East Germany 2-0 and Brazil 2-0) in entertaining style, captain Johan Cruyff, Johnny Repp and Johan Neeskens constantly shifting and changing to bewilder the opposition and thrill the watching fans. But they were dangerously tight in defence too, having conceded only one goal in six games.

West Germany, despite having notched up an impressive 11-goal tally in the opening rounds, had nevertheless shown their slight vulnerability at the back by conceding three. But it was too tight to call, and the final clash was a mouth-watering prospect.

The final could not have had a more dramatic start. Straight from the kick-off, Holland played the ball straight into the German goal area, Cruyff was brought down by Hoeness, and Neeskens nervelessly converted the first penalty ever awarded in a World Cup final, and recorded the fastest-ever final goal.

Holland continued to dominate, both in possession and

territory, although the threat of a German counter-attack from defence could never be discounted, thanks mostly to the genius of captain Franz Beckenbauer (affectionately nicknamed 'The Kaiser') to spot and make openings from deep positions, and the willingness of strikers like Gerd Müller and Bernd Holzenbein to run forever and make space up front.

It was one of those moves which put the Germans back in the game, and the tackle on Holzenbein by Jansen in the Dutch area was deemed worthy of another penalty which Beckenbauer's Bayern Munich club-mate, Paul Breitner, slotted into the net.

It was all over just before half time. In the 43rd minute, Müller evaded his Dutch attendants to whip home his 68th - and last - goal for his nation. The Germans then shut up shop, successfully stopped Holland with all the tightness and discipline for which they were justly famous, and became world champions.

The answer to that second question, then, also appeared to be 'No'.

Franco Cedes Power To Juan Carlos

JULY 19

The first signs that General Francisco Franco's 48-year reign as dictator of Spain was finally reaching its end came today in the capital Madrid, when the 81-year-old *Caudillo* (the title he took as Head of State for life in 1947) temporarily relinquished control of the country to his designated successor, Prince Juan Carlos, heir to the Spanish throne.

Franco's move came amid growing political and industrial unrest, increased attacks by Basque separatist guerrillas, and fears that even more serious political and civil violence could erupt.

Franco, who had nominated Prince Juan Carlos as his chosen heir five years ago, would resume command in September, and remain in power until his death in 1975.

Argentina Welcomes President Isabel

ISABEL PERÓN (pictured right) became Argentina's first woman President today, following the death of her husband, Juan Domingo Perón (pictured left), at the age of 78. She also followed in the footsteps of Perón's first wife, popularly known as Evita, whose life story would become the basis for the Tim Rice-Andrew Lloyd Webber musical *Evita* nearly a quarter of a century later.

Juan Perón was a key figure in post-war Argentina, serving as President from 1946 to 1955 and again from 1973 to 1974. Impressed by European fascist governments, he brooked no opposition to his own style of rule, though he gained the sympathies of Argentina's poor, the so-called 'shirtless ones', for his social reforms. However, when his economic programmes ran out of steam in the mid-1950s he was deposed by a coup and fled to exile in Spain.

Perón returned to Argentina in 1971 and became its President in 1973, with Isabel as his Vice-President. With the economy deteriorating, producing record inflation in 1975 and 1976, the writing was on the wall for the last Perón government and Isabel would be deposed in a military coup in March 1976.

Mama Cass Weighs Out

US pop star Mama Cass Elliot died today in the London flat of fellow singer Harry Nilsson, where she'd been staying with her road-manager. Two days before, she had completed a successful two-week residency at the London Palladium, and was on the verge of establishing herself as a solo star after finding 1960s fame with The Mamas and the Papas, whose major hits included *Monday*, *Monday* and *California Dreamin'*.

Though morbid press speculation on the cause of her death ranged from drug abuse to choking on a sandwich, the pathologist's report concluded that her fatal heart attack was due to her obesity. At 225 pounds, the singer – still only in her early thirties – weighed nearly twice the average for a woman of her height.

Player Wins Fourth Grand Slam Event

The winner of the British Open today at Royal Lytham, South African golfer Gary Player became one of only four men – the others being Gene Sarazen, Ben Hogan and Jack Nicklaus – to have captured all four titles in the modern Grand Slam.

Player won the British Open three times (in 1959, 1968 and 1974), the US Masters twice (in 1961 and 1974) and the PGA Tournament twice (1962 and 1972). When he won the US Open in 1965 he became the first non-American player to take that title since Englishman Ted Ray in 1920.

UK TOP 10 SINGLES

1: She
- Charles Aznavour
2: Kissin' In The Back Row Of The Movies
- The Drifters
3: Bangin' Man
- Slade
4: Rock Your Baby
- George McCrae
5: I'd Love You To Want Me
- Lobo
6: Young Girl
- Gary Puckett & The Union Gap
7: Band On The Run
- Paul McCartney & Wings
8: Always Yours
- Gary Glitter
9: Banana Rock
- The Wombles
10: Wall Street Shuffle
- 10cc

JULY 24

Nixon Impeached After Supreme Court Orders Tapes Surrender

THE WATERGATE SCANDAL reached a new and decisive phase in Washington today when the US Supreme Court ruled unanimously against President Nixon, who had sought to block the release - to the House Judiciary Committee - of White House tapes relating to the break-in and subsequent cover-up activities. The court insisted Watergate was a criminal matter, and that the President's claim that national security was involved did not apply.

The situation worsened for the President on July 30 when the Judiciary Committee - whose public hearings had first disclosed evidence of illegal activities in the White House - recommended that President Nixon be impeached on three counts: obstruction of justice, abuse of presidential powers, and trying to impede the impeachment process by defying committee subpoenas.

Two other possible counts – Nixon's unauthorized, secret bombing of Cambodia in 1969, and use of public funds to improve his private property – were rejected. That was small consolation for the finally cornered Chief Executive. On August 8 he would become the first President of the United States to resign, his bluff called and his stonewalling ended.

JULY 6

Love-Match For Evert And Connors

US tennis ace Jimmy Connors was riding high when he beat 39-year-old Ken Rosewall 6-1, 6-1, 6-4 in the men's final at Wimbledon today, for it was a year in which the brash young star won three of the four Grand Slam Tournaments – the others being the US, Australian and French Opens.

It was also the year in which he and fellow American Chris Evert became engaged in a love-match that delighted press and public alike, although both would eventually marry other partners.

The photogenic pair pulled off a double first at Wimbledon, with Evert beating Olga Morozova in the women's final – an unexpected win, since her opponent had already beaten the legendary Billie Jean King 6-0, 6-4 *en route* to their Centre Court clash.

JULY 24

Greek Colonels Bow To Democracy

Seven years of military rule ended in popular rejoicing on the streets of Athens today when the armed forces junta stepped down. It had been defeated by domestic economic problems and a renewed crisis in Cyprus which had seen Greek-born EOKA sympathizers combine with Cyprus National Guard officers to launch an unsuccessful *coup d'état* against President Makarios.

Governmental control passed into civilians hands, and the move prompted a return from exile of left-wing leader Andreas Papandreou and former premier Constantine Karamanlis, the latter sworn in as head of a coalition government. There was speculation at the time that King Constantine might also return to the throne, but in a referendum the new republic voted against such a move.

AUGUST 9

Disgraced Nixon Quits, Ford Sworn In As President

GERALD RUDOLPH FORD, was sworn in as the thirty-eighth President of the United States today after a disgraced Richard Nixon resigned to avoid almost certain impeachment for his complicity in the Watergate affair and its cover-up aftermath. Ford was the first man to become US President without having fought a national election, his appointment as Vice-President by Nixon in 1973 having followed the resignation of Spiro Agnew after accusations of bribery and failure to pay income tax.

Ford, aged 60, had a reputation as an easygoing conservative. He appointed the Governor of New York, Nelson Rockefeller – another reputedly moderate Republican – as Vice-President.

With both the elected President and former Vice-President since discredited, Ford's first and most formidable task was to try to regain the trust of the American people who, for the last two years, had been subjected to the undignified spectacle of untrustworthy politicians engaged in a major scandal.

Re-elected President with an overwhelming majority in 1972, Nixon's fortunes were not affected by the arrest of five burglars attempting to bug the Democratic Party campaign headquarters in the Watergate office and hotel complex in Washington. The President had consistently refused to admit any knowledge of the 'dirty tricks' exercise and had steadfastly maintained his innocence, despite the relentless amount of evidence which piled up to implicate him.

Unable to count on enough supporting votes in the House Judiciary Committee threatening to impeach him for 'high crimes and misdemeanours', Nixon's resignation became inevitable on August 2 when John Dean and John Ehrlichman, two of his closest aides, were sentenced to four and five-year prison terms respectively for their involvement in the Watergate cover-up.

Wounded Knee Trial Erupts In Violence

The trial in Minneapolis-St Paul of American Indian civil-rights leaders for last year's occupation of the Wounded Knee Reservation in South Dakota was reduced to a shambles today when police used mace (tear-gas) to quell courtroom demonstrators and arrested two defence lawyers.

The lawyers were held for contempt of court when they objected to the method of cross-examination used on a major witness for the prosecution and refused Judge Fred Nichol's request to allow the case to continue.

Angola's Agony Nearly Over?

Portugal today announced its intention to give its African colony of Angola independence, the change to take place over a two-year period.

The transition would not be without its problems.

There were three separate groups fighting for Angola's independence, the MPLA, UNITA and FNLA - all with differing visions of their country's future.

The MPLA was the most radical, and had the support of the Soviet Union to train its troops in Marxist philosophy.

Two other Portuguese colonies, Mozambique and Guinea-Bissau, also held out hopes of independence as Portugal's political climate moved steadily leftwards.

Police And Hippies Fight It Out

In an incident truly worthy of the British press's so-called 'silly season', police and festival-goers fought an eight-hour running battle at an illegal pop festival in Windsor Great Park today.

The annual Festivals of the People, as they were known, were intended as a reaction to the increasing commercialization of music, but their proximity to the Queen's residence, Windsor Castle, was always going to be a problem.

Six hundred police broke up the festival after those attending refused to leave.

The poet Heathcote Williams would later unsuccessfully sue the local police commissioner for 'loss of faith in the police'.

UK TOP 10 SINGLES

1: Living Doll
- Cliff Richard
2: Dream Lover
- Bobby Darin
3: Battle Of New Orleans
- Lonnie Donegan
4: Lipstick On Your Collar
- Connie Francis
5: Lonely Boy
- Paul Anka
6: Big Hunk O' Love
- Elvis Presley
7: A Teenager In Love
- Marty Wilde
8: Roulette
- Russ Conway
9: The Heart Of A Man
- Frankie Vaughan
10: Only Sixteen
- Craig Douglas

ARRIVALS

Born this month:
8: Brian Harvey, UK pop
star (East 17)

DEPARTURES

Died this month:
6: Gene 'Jug' Ammons, US
jazz saxophonist, aged 49
13: Kate O'Brian, Irish
playwright and novelist,
aged 76
22: Dr Jacob Bronowski,
UK biologist, aged 66
26: Charles Lindbergh,
record-breaking American
aviator, aged 72 *(see Came
& Went pages)*

Turkey Invades Cyprus

ONLY TWO WEEKS AFTER the Greek and Turkish foreign ministers signed a peace deal and new constitution for Cyprus - the Mediterranean island divided by loyalties to both countries - with British Foreign Secretary James Callaghan in Geneva, Turkish Army tanks rolled into the streets of the Greek Cypriot northern port of Famagusta today, linking up with land forces which had battled their way from their headquarters in Kyrenia.

An estimated 12,000 Greek Cypriots were reported to be fleeing Famagusta as Turkish airforce jets used napalm and high explosives to blast the port and leave the way clear for the army advance. Many of the civilians sought refuge in the nearby British military base in Dhekelia.

The present, most serious crisis began with the attempted dawn coup of July 15, staged by Greek officers of the National Guard who supported union with Greece. It forced the escape into exile of President Archbishop Makarios, and all subsequent efforts to seek a peaceful solution to the dispute had failed.

The two national factions had been at odds since Cyprus gained independence from Britain in 1960, but today's massive invasion would see the island permanently divided by a so-called 'Green Line', with many Greeks losing their homes and possessions in the now Turkish-occupied North, and Turks dispossessed in the Greek-controlled South.

40,000 British Tourists Stranded

More than 40,000 British holiday-makers found themselves stranded in European resorts today when the package holiday group, Court Line, collapsed with heavy debts.

Although British Trade Secretary Peter Shore gave assurances that everyone caught up in the company's failure would be flown home, there were another 100,000 people who were unlikely to see their money again. They had also booked vacations with Court Line, which also owned the major holiday firms, Clarksons and Horizon.

Gaddafi Arrests Egyptian Troops

In Libya, Colonel Gaddafi's forces arrested 500 Egyptian soldiers today in a tit-for-tat row over Egypt's refusal to return 40 Libyan air force planes located at an Egyptian airbase.

Gaddafi, who assumed power in 1969 following a military coup which deposed King Idris, had a reputation as a wayward, hard-line politician. His actions today only confirmed that. Relations with Egypt would worsen over the following years, resulting in the four-day Libyan-Egyptian War in 1977.

Colonel Gaddafi's aggressive attitude to Western governments would also eventually result in the controversial American air-strike against suspected terrorist bases within Libya in April 1986 after Western intelligence services claimed they had proof that Gaddafi had funded an anti-US bombing campaign in Europe.

WACKY WOMBLES WOW UK WECORD-BUYERS

When a TV production company secured the rights to make an animated series based on Elizabeth Beresford's best-selling children's books about The Wombles - a breed of cuddly underground critters whose life-long task was to clean up and recycle the rubbish they found above ground on Wimbledon Common, South-West London - they would have reason to thank the lucky stars which inspired them to ask composer-arranger Mike Batt to write a theme and incidental music.

Swept up by characteristic enthusiasm, the Southampton-born Batt began to think bigger and, drawing on his skills as an arranger - and a man cursed/blessed with a wacky sense of humour - he extended his brief and put together a collection of pop pastiche songs about the Wombles, or using the expression 'Wombling' in their titles or lyrics.

Taking them to the CBS subsidiary Epic Records in London, Mike Batt was snapped up to begin two years of inspired and very successful lunacy for him, the record company - and the TV series, which benefited from a rush of unexpected and ratings-boosting publicity.

Five big hits were scored by The Wombles in Britain and Europe this year (America resisted the joke, despite a couple of visits by a Womble-suited Batt to appear on US TV shows). January brought us *The Wombling Song,* the series theme tune, which became the country's No 4 single. April brought the No 3 hit *Remember You're A Womble* (as if we could!), while June's *Banana Rock* peaked at No 16.

The relative lack of success of Minuetto Allegretto, a maybe too-clever classical music piece which did no better than No 16, was cancelled out at year end when *Wombling*

Merry Christmas was December's No 2 stocking filler for young and old.

There would be three more UK Top 30 hits in 1975 (*Wombling White Tie And Tails, Super Womble* and *Let's Womble To The Party Tonight*) before Mike Batt wisely called it a day and moved on to other, more serious things, including composing the music soundtrack for the animated film of *Watership Down,* in the course of which he wrote and produced Art Garfunkel's huge hit *Bright Eyes.*

Still successfully combining careers as a songwriter, arranger, score composer, and record producer, Mike Batt has no reason to feel anything but pride for The Wombles - a rare burst of silly but very clever fun in an all-too-serious world.

McCARTNEY WINS GREEN CARD BATTLE

Repeatedly unsuccessful in his attempts to gain the so-called 'green card' visa-cum-work permit without which he could not tour the US with his band, Wings, Paul McCartney finally received clearance from US Immigration authorities this April and could start to plan his first American tour since The Beatles split up in 1970.

McCartney's failure to get clearance was due to marijuana possession offences in his past (twice in 1972 - while on tour in Sweden and at the McCartney farmhouse on Scotland's Mull of Kintyre), although his inability to tour had not seemed to have affected sales of his albums and singles in the US.

In 1973, for instance, the single *Hi Hi Hi* had reached the US Top 10, while the *Red Rose Speedway* album had topped the US charts at the same time as his *My Love* single held the US top spot, with *Live And Let Die* - his theme song for the new James Bond movie - repeating the feat in August.

But the need to get to America was heightened by the new Wings album *Band On The Run*. Recorded in Nigeria at the end of 1973, at studios owned by former Cream drummer Ginger Baker, it was the best thing McCartney had so far created, and he wanted to ensure it had all the help he could give it.

Released in April, the *Band On The Run* album went straight to No 1 in the US, eventually selling six million copies. By June the title track single was also the US No 1, just as McCartney arrived in Nashville for his first-ever recording sessions in the New World, which now lay at his feet, ready for conquering properly.

ROXY WRAP-UP AS US SHUNS SCANTIES

Although firmly established as one of the world's most popular, inventive and successful rock bands by the beginning of 1974, Britain's Roxy Music were still finding the US strangely resistant to their unqie appeal.

Their 1973 smash hit album *For Your Pleasure,* for instance, while hitting the Top 10 of some 15 countries, had only wheezed its way to a lowly No 193 in the US Top 200 album chart, while lead singer Bryan Ferry's first solo album, *These Foolish Things,* had failed to reach that US chart at all!

In June, Roxy Music hit the US tour circuit for only the second time, and while that clearly helped sales of their *Stranded* album - a UK and European No 1 - it was only to the extent that it inched its way to No 186.

After a triumphant sell-out British tour in October, and a UK Top 20 appearance with *All I Want Is You,* the instant hit status of the band's new album, *Country Life* (which went straight into the UK chart at No 3), must have given them reason for optimism about its US potential.

That was soon smashed. The jungle-set sleeve of *Country Life* featured two scantily-clad models who proved too much for US distributors' sensitivities. Without time to

The Wombles

change the artwork, *Country Life* was sold in the US with an extremely attractive and eye-catching (not!) opaque green shrink-wrap hiding (shock! horror!) the girls.

All was not lost, however. When Roxy Music's 1975 world tour hit the US in February, *Country Life* finally gave them the beginning of a breakthrough there when it finally reached No 37 in the national charts. It had been a long haul.

Official - Aerosols Harm Ozone Layer

Early indications that the use of aerosol sprays was harming the environment were published in the influential American magazine *Science* this month.

According to the article by two American researchers, Steven Wofsy and Michael McElroy, the gases used in aerosols had been found to travel between 10 and 15 miles up into the stratosphere, where they broke down the natural ozone - a form of oxygen which forms a layer around the earth and absorbs the sun's harmful ultraviolet radiation.

The researchers predicted that, at the present rate, 15 per cent of the ozone layer would be destroyed by the end of the century. Despite warnings that the erosion of the earth's protection would raise the incidence of skin cancer and lead to environmental changes, companies using the harmful Freon gases to power aerosols dismissed the report as 'largely hypothesis'. Unfortunately, history would prove those companies wrong.

BBC Offers Text On Television

The BBC today unveiled *Ceefax*, a television text display system utilizing one of the 40 spare lines that the British 625-line system did not need to carry TV pictures. The service would soon be developed to include information as diverse as football results, the weather and horoscopes. Though the system used was developed separately from the similar *Oracle*, devised by Independent Television, the two rivals would work together to further the British-pioneered technology.

Ethiopian Coup Overthrows Haile Selassie

THE 58-YEAR RULE of Emperor Haile Selassie of Ethiopia came to a close today as the man known to his subjects as King of Kings and Lion of Judah quit the royal palace in the capital, Addis Ababa, overthrown in a bloodless coup staged by a group of middle-ranking army officers.

His departure was in less than the regal style he so loved - he occupied the back seat of a Volkswagen that had seen better days.

Born Ras Tafari in 1892, the emperor adopted his title 'Haile Selassie' ('Might of the Trinity') when he took the throne in 1930. When his country, then known as Abyssinia, was invaded by Italy in 1935 and he was refused League of Nations help, he went into exile in Britain, only returning to Ethiopia in 1941.

Selassie stood accused by his opponents of allowing widespread corruption and failing to deal with the severe poverty of his subjects. His exiled son, Crown Prince Asfa Wossen, was invited to return to the country as king, but with no political power. The new military regime subsequently developed strong links with the USSR.

Cher In Life-Saving Action

Prompt action by American pop singer **Cher** was said to have saved the life of Alan Gorrie, bass-player with the Scottish rock group The Average White Band, at a show-business party which followed the group's showcase performance at the Los Angeles Troubadour tonight.

Heroin had apparently been circulated at the party in the guise of cocaine and, tragically, claimed the life of another group member, 24-year-old drummer Robbie McIntosh.

Cher, who declined the drug ('I can't even take aspirin,' she commented), was an innocent bystander – but she had the presence of mind to revive Gorrie with the 'kiss of life'.

UK TOP 10 SINGLES

1: Kung Fu Fighting
- Carl Douglas
2: Love Me For A Reason
- The Osmonds
3: Annie's Song
- John Denver
4: Y Viva España
- Sylvia
5: I'm Leaving It (All) Up To You
- Donny & Marie Osmond
6: Hang On In There Baby
- Johnny Bristol
7: You You You
- Alvin Stardust
8: When Will I See You Again
- The Three Degrees
9: What Becomes Of The Broken Hearted
- Jimmy Ruffin
10: Queen Of Clubs
- KC & The Sunshine Band

Born this month:
18: Sol Campbell, England Under-21 international football player
20: Julian Joachim, England Under-21 international football player

DEPARTURES

Died this month:
4: Creighton Abrams, US military commander, aged 60
16: 'Phog' Allen (Forrest Clare Allen), US basketball coaching legend (University of Kansas 1908-54, US Olympic team 1952), aged 89
21: Walter Brennan, US Academy Award-winning character actor (*Kentucky, Come And Get It, The Westerner, Bad Day At Black Rock, Rio Bravo, How The West Was Won*, etc.), aged 80

First Female Cop-Show Hits US TV Screens

The world's first television series about a woman police officer, the American-made *Policewoman,* made its debut broadcast via the NBC network today. Voted a hit by critics and viewers, the series starred Angie Dickinson as Sgt. 'Pepper' Anderson and used real cases for its story-lines.

Dickinson, the sometime wife of songwriter Burt Bacharach, made the show her springboard to big-screen stardom. The success of *Policewoman* would encourage other TV producers to feature female leads in police dramas. The genre soon expanded to include the ultimate female cop duo in *Cagney And Lacey.*

SEPT

Ford Pardons 'Ailing' Nixon And Draft-Dodgers

Disgraced former President Nixon was granted an unconditional pardon by his successor, President Gerald Ford, today. The pardon, which was as widely anticipated as it was condemned by a number of key political commentators, meant that Nixon would now not face charges for his part in the Watergate scandal.

In magnanimous mood, the President also pardoned all American draft-dodgers who evaded call-up during the Vietnam War. Many who had spent years in enforced exile because of their opposition to the war were now free to return home without fear of arrest and imprisonment.

The decision to pardon Nixon was one which President Ford hoped would avoid further anguish to both Nixon and the American people. His health said to be in rapid decline since his resignation, Nixon would soon afterwards be admitted to hospital with a suspected blood clot in his leg.

Unemployment Versus Inflation

GIVING BRITAIN a foretaste of what would prove the Conservative Party's guiding principle in the 1980s, right-wing Tory politician Sir Keith Joseph today threw his weight behind a monetarism policy - the control of an economy by restricting the money supply - as the best weapon to fight rising inflation, and dismissed the ideal of full employment as being both unachievable and maybe unacceptable.

Leader of the Opposition Edward Heath disagreed fundamentally and vehemently with Sir Keith, who was his shadow Home Secretary. Pressed to comment on Sir Keith's remarks, Mr Heath confirmed that he still believed that large-scale unemployment was a 'greater social evil' than inflation.

In October, Sir Keith would create more controversy when he used a speaking engagement to suggest that one solution to the unemployment problem could be to improve birth control among lower-income families.

Portugal's Spinola Resigns

Portugal's President Spinola stepped down from office today, only five months after seizing power in a coup, issuing dire warnings that the country was 'heading for a precipice'. Political turmoil within Portugal had recently increased as left-wing politicians gained popular support, and General Spinola felt unable to reconcile the demands of the radical Armed Forces Movement with what he believed to be best for the people of Portugal.

'My sense of loyalty', he explained, 'prevents me from betraying my people, for whom new forms of slavery are being prepared under the flag of a false freedom.'

Spinola was succeeded by General Francisco de Costa Gomes, with whom he had worked closely over the past few months.

OCT

OCTOBER 5

Five Killed In Guildford As IRA Terrorizes British Mainland

A month of intensified IRA bombing on the British mainland was highlighted by horrific events tonight in the Surrey market town of Guildford, when five people died and 65 were seriously injured in bomb attacks on two pubs, both well known as regular hang-outs for military personnel based in the area.

On October 11, two further bombs exploded in the Central London areas of Pall Mall and Marble Arch, while a third was detonated on October 22 near the London home of Opposition leader Edward Heath. The last attack, on October 28, saw a bomb explode under the car of Denis Howell, the Sports Minister. Mr Howell

was, fortunately, not in the car at the time.

An intensive search for the pub bombers would lead to the eventual arrest, trial and conviction of the so-called Guildford Four. Their sentences would be overturned some 15 years later as 'unsafe', and dramatized in the film *In The Name Of The Father*.

Labour Wins Snap Election And Working Majority

FOLLOWING THE SECOND general election of the year, Britain's Labour government today had the clear working majority it had been Prime Minister Harold Wilson's intention to win for himself to ensure that he and his team could govern effectively without constant reference to, and deals with, minority parties holding the balance of power in crucial parliamentary votes.

But it was an 'only just' majority of three – enough, said the victorious Prime Minister, to make his position 'viable'.

Although back in power, Mr Wilson did not pose for the usual victory photos outside 10 Downing Street, the British premier's traditional residence. He had - in March this year - taken the unusual decision of abandoning Downing Street, preferring instead to live in his own home in Westminster's Lord North Street. Explaining his move, Mr Wilson had said, 'I don't want to live above the shop any more.'

His decision was brought into question on October 25 when, in a strange echo of the Watergate break-in which had just led to the resignation of US President Nixon, tax papers and other personal documents were stolen from the house.

Conspiracy theorists' suggestions that the burglary was part of a right-wing plot to discredit Mr Wilson were supported by the apparently professional nature of the raid, with elements of M.I.5. hot favourites for blame.

UK TOP 10 SINGLES

1: Sad Sweet Dreamer
- Sweet Sensation

2: Annie's Song
- John Denver

3: Gee Baby
- Peter Shelley

4: Rock Me Gently
- Andy Kim

5: Everything I Own
- Ken Boothe

6: Long Tall Glasses
- Leo Sayer

7: Kung Fu Fighting
- Carl Douglas

8: Hang On In There Baby
- Johnny Bristol

9: Far Far Away
- Slade

10: I Get A Kick Out Of You
- Gary Shearston

Liverpool's Conteh Wins World Boxing Title

In a month which saw more than one boxing crown change hands (*see main story*), Liverpudlian boxer John Conteh tonight won the world light heavyweight title in a fight against his Argentinian opponent, Jorge Ahumada – so becoming the first British fighter to hold the title since Freddie Mills won it 25 years ago.

In a fight which lasted the full 15 rounds, Conteh eventually won on points. He would not go on to establish himself as the world-class prospect this famous victory had made him appear, however, and his hardest victory would eventually be against a serious drinking problem which would come with local fame.

Maze Prison Riot Spreads To Streets

Ulster's high-security Maze Prison was set alight by Republican prisoners tonight as an act of defiance against new restrictions on visiting rights.
Troops were called in to support prison guards and, when news of the disturbance spread, crowds lit bonfires in streets in the Catholic area of Belfast to begin a night of serious civil unrest.

DEPARTURES

Died this month:
4: Anne Sexton, American poet, aged 46
13: Ed Sullivan, American TV variety show host, aged 72
24: David Oistrakh, Russian violinist, aged 66
25: Nick Drake, British folk-singer, songwriter *(see main story)*, aged 26

OCTOBER 29

Ali Wins 'Rumble In The Jungle' To Reclaim Crown

IN KINSHASA, ZAIRE, tonight Muhammad Ali became only the second boxer to make a comeback and retake the world heavyweight title when he won the fight billed by its promoters as 'The Rumble in the Jungle' by knocking out fellow-American George Foreman after just eight of 15 scheduled rounds.

Roared on by more than 60,000 fans, Ali - clearly the firm favourite - used a unique and dangerous fight-plan to regain his crown. For seven rounds he soaked up a pounding from Foreman with barely a reply shot. Ali, it transpired, had trained as a human punching-bag, building the stamina he knew he'd need to survive before Foreman's own stamina ran out, enabling Ali to go on the offensive.

The 32-year-old from Louisville, Kentucky, may no longer have been able to say - as he did in his early career - that he could 'float like a butterfly, sting like a bee'. But his victory tonight proved he was still incredibly tough, still capable of knocking out the biggest, and still able to outsmart the best.

OCTOBER 3

Come In, Number Ten!

Brazilian football legend Pelé - born Edson Arantes do Nascimento, in 1940 - played his last game for Santos, his only professional club for 18 years, tonight.

The superstar striker, acknowledged as one of the world's most gifted and inventive players of all time, played the first 20 minutes of a match against Ponte Preta and left the pitch, in tears, to a standing ovation. The club then ceremonially retired the number 10 team-position Pelé had graced since his debut in 1956, declaring the number was never to be used on a player's shirt again.

The Brazilian ace would, however, be tempted out of retirement in 1975, when he signed a $4.5 million contract to enjoy a two-year swansong with New York Cosmos in the North American Soccer League.

OCTOBER 17

Americans Told, 'Wash In Cold Water'

The continuing fuel crisis caused by the Arab States' year-long oil sales embargo prompted President Gerald Ford's call today for Americans to use cold water to wash, and to reduce car use by 5 per cent.

The embargo was imposed in response to the US' support for Israel in the 1973 Arab-Israeli War. Saudi Arabia, Bahrain, Libya, Qatar and Kuwait all ceased oil exports to the States, this cut US supply by 20 per cent, causing the price at US petrol pumps to rise, and long lines of impatient motorists.

OCTOBER 25

Bedsit Bard Dead At Twenty-Six

Nick Drake, the British folk-singer who became the voice of the disenchanted young and a generation of student bedsit dwellers, was found dead in bed at his parents' Tamworth home this morning. He had taken an overdose of prescribed anti-depressants, though no intention to kill himself was ever established. He was 26. Drake, the brother of film and stage actress Gabrielle Drake, would be credited by many later artists as a major influence. When his producer and close friend Joe Boyd sold the rights to his recordings to Island Records, it was with the proviso that they never be deleted. They never have been.

CHARLES LINDBERGH - THE LAST GREAT AMERICAN HERO

It's hard to think of Charles Lindbergh, who finally succumbed to leukemia today at the age of 72, as anything but the grim-jawed, lean, handsome and young aviator whose astonishing - and astonishingly brave - non-stop solo flight across the Atlantic in 1927 literally grabbed world headlines and made him an international star.

Sadly, tragically, Lindbergh's fame also made him and his family a target for less savoury attention, and in 1932 he and his wife would suffer a terrible blow when their young son was kidnapped and murdered. Hounded by tabloid press, the couple were forced to seek the refuge of a period of exile in Britain in 1935.

Born in Detroit and the son of a liberal Republican congressman, Lindbergh became an officer in the US Army Air Corps (USAAC) Reserve in 1925. While the vast (for the times) $25,000 reward on offer for beating the Atlantic solo was undoubtedly a consideration in Lindbergh's 1927 flight in the Spirit Of St Louis, it was also the type of challenge he relished. The ticker-tape welcome which greeted his return to New York after his pioneering 3,600 mile, 33 hour flight was the least he could have expected.

Already an adviser to US Airlines, Lindbergh and his wife flew many survey flights for the company over the Arctic, North Pacific and North Atlantic while he rose to the rank of colonel with the USAAC.

While in Britain after his son's death, Lindbergh was invited to Germany by Goering to inspect the German air force, the Luftwaffe. Impressed by what he'd seen of Nazi Germany, Lindbergh returned to the US to actively campaign against American foreign policy, although the Japanese attack on Pearl Harbor spurred him into involvement in the US war effort, when he helped improve warplanes and flew a number of missions in the Pacific.

A talented engineer, Lindbergh was a senior technical consultant to Pan American Airways after the war, and also invented a pump for a mechanical heart. A committed conservationist towards the end of his life, and by now bearing the rank of Brigadier-General, Lindbergh became active in the World Wildlife Fund - a contribution to society he felt was probably the greatest of his life.

To the rest of us, however, those 33 hours between May 20 and May 22, 1927, were the reason we remember him best, and why he has his indelible place in the history books.

MARCH 28
ARTHUR 'BIG BOY' CRUDUP - VICTIM OF THE SYSTEM

While it would be an exaggeration to say that without Arthur 'Big Boy' Crudup, the Mississippi-born blues singer who died today at the age of 69, there would have been no rock 'n' roll, the fact remains that Elvis Presley's decision to record three Crudup songs - *That's Alright Mama*, *My Baby Left Me* and *So Glad You're Mine* - would prove a landmark at a time when white boys just didn't sing black music.

But it is no exaggeration to say that Crudup remains a prime example of the way in which the white-owned music business systematically ripped off the black musicians whose work they drew on to create that immensely lucrative hybrid. Despite the millions of copies Presley's versions of his songs must have sold between 1954 and this year, the system would conspire to keep his financial reward negligible - Arthur Crudup would be penniless when he died after a stroke in the North Hampton-Accomac Memorial Hospital in Nassawadox, Virginia.

Crudup did not actually record until 1942, when he - like so many Southern blacks - arrived in Chicago looking for work. A big man (hence his nickname), he'd made his living as a logger, truck driver, sawmill hand and farmer, but his reputation as a distinctive, harsh and high-voiced singer, and a good guitarist.

Until he was signed to record for the Victor Company, Crudup lived in a wooden crate under Chicago's elevated railway and played for pennies from passers-by. Success with *Rock Me Mama* and the three songs Elvis Presley would hear on the radio as a young man - and use to make his first huge impact as a recording artist - ensured that Crudup's reputation was made and he was able to become a full-time professional musician.

He did tour Europe on a few occasions in the late 1950s and early 1960s, but his real reward - and his rightful due - never came his way, despite his efforts to gain justice.

NOV

PLO Chief Yasir Arafat Addresses UN

THE UNITED NATIONS formally recognized the Palestine Liberation Organization (PLO), formed in 1964, as the legitimate government of Palestine today, when Yasir Arafat (pictured) - the PLO's head since 1969 - was allowed to address the UN General Assembly for the first time.

Clearly emotional, Arafat told delegates, 'I have come bearing an olive branch and a freedom fighter's gun. Do not let the olive branch fall from my hands'. The gun, in fact, was strapped to his waist.

The tolerance shown to Arafat was not appreciated by more than 100,000 demonstrators outside the UN's headquarters in New York, who protested against the PLO being allowed to participate in the Middle-East debate.

Their suspicions about Arafat's apparent conversion to a more conciliatory approach appeared well-founded ten days later, when Palestinian hijackers killed a West German banker in Tunis and held 27 others, demanding the release of prisoners in Egypt.

NOVEMBER 24

Ford's Nuclear Accord

Months of painstaking negotiations by US Secretary of State Henry Kissinger paid off today when President Gerald Ford and Soviet leader Leonid Brezhnev reached an agreement to limit their countries' strategic nuclear weapons systems.

The US policy of *détente*, fostered by Ford's predecessor Richard Nixon, was a response to the uncontrolled build-up of weapons by East and West to the point at which both superpowers possessed the capability to destroy each other many times over.

After what was his first meeting with the Soviet leader, Ford reported that they now had 'a sound basis for a new agreement that will constrain our military competition over the next decade'.

NOVEMBER 13

Final Curtain For Actor/Director De Sica

Vittorio de Sica, the noted film director and actor, died today at the age of 72. Well known in his native Italy in the 1930s, he only found world fame after World War II, through films like the Academy Award-winning *Shoeshine* in 1946 and *Bicycle Thieves* two years later, both of which he directed.

British readers may remember him as an actor in the 1959 TV series *The Four Just Men*.

NOVEMBER 26

Pioneer 11 Reaches Jupiter

The US space probe *Pioneer 11*, launched from Cape Canaveral in April 1973, drew near enough to the planet Jupiter this month to send photographs back to Earth. After completing this stage of its trip, *Pioneer 11* would travel on to Saturn where, in 1975, it would send back the very first observations of the planet which revealed Saturn's eleventh moon and two new rings.

By the mid-1990s the spacecraft will have travelled a staggering 4 billion miles from Earth, its signals taking six hours to reach scientists at NASA control. Although its longevity has astonished space experts, its power source is failing.

Once out of range the craft will follow its sister ship, *Pioneer 10* - now even further away - into outer space, carrying NASA's famous 'visiting-card'. This shows a diagram of the hydrogen atom, a map locating our sun, and a naked man and woman, hands raised in greeting, to any extraterrestrials it might encounter.

UK TOP 10 SINGLES

1: Gonna Make You A Star
- David Essex
2: Killer Queen
- Queen
3: Everything I Own
- Ken Boothe
4: (Hey There) Lonely Girl
- Eddie Holman
5: All Of Me Loves All Of You
- The Bay City Rollers
6: You're The First, The Last, My Everything
- Barry White
7: Far Far Away
- Slade
8: Down On The Beach Tonight
- The Drifters
9: Let's Put It All Together
- The Stylistics
10: Let's Get Together Again
- The Glitter Band

Many Killed As IRA Bombers Hit Birmingham And Woolwich

NOVEMBER 21

Seventeen people died this evening when the IRA exploded bombs in two popular Birmingham pubs, the Mulberry Bush and the Tavern in the Town. The two packed pubs were reduced to rubble and nearly 120 people were admitted to hospital with serious injuries.

This latest escalation in violence seemed to be the IRA's revenge for the British Government's prohibition of a hero's funeral planned for James McDade, killed the previous week while planting a bomb in the nearby city of Coventry.

The Birmingham attack followed that on a Woolwich, London, pub on November 7 in which one person was killed and 28 were injured. On November 29, the British Government would act against the IRA, when the Prevention of Terrorism Act became law, enabling police to hold suspected terrorists without charge for a much longer time than other laws allowed.

Footnote: As with the Guildford pub bombings of last month, the convictions that followed the Birmingham outrages would be overturned many years later.

NOVEMBER 12

'Lucky' Lord Lucan Disappears After Nanny's Murder

A MASSIVE BRITISH MANHUNT, which would soon become an international search, began tonight in London when the estranged wife of Richard John Bingham, the seventh Earl of Lucan, fled her Belgravia house and burst into a nearby pub shouting, 'He's murdered my nanny! My children, my children!'

Police called to the scene found Sandra Rivett, the nanny who looked after the couple's children, brutally murdered. Lady Lucan alleged that a man she believed to be her husband had also attacked her in the dark. Lord Lucan himself had disappeared.

A direct descendant of one of the British commanders whose rivalry and bungling caused the disastrous Charge of the Light Brigade at Balaclava during the Crimean War in 1854, Lord Lucan was a notorious gambler known as 'Lucky' in the smart society circles in which he moved. A number of Lucan's wealthy friends were questioned by police during their enquiries, but no real progress was made after his car was found abandoned near the English coast.

Although there would be numerous reported sightings of Lord Lucan around the world through the years, he was never apprehended. He would remain a wanted man after an inquest jury ruled that he had, in fact, killed Sandra Rivett.

NOVEMBER 22

Helen's Five-Day Reign Ends In Tears

Helen Morgan, the United Kingdom's representative in this year's Miss World beauty contest, was crowned tonight in London knowing that, for the first time, the event was being televised live and that her victory was being watched by millions of viewers at home.

Her reign was to last just five days, however, and was ended when it was learned that Helen was, in fact, an unmarried mother.

The title was subsequently handed down to second-placed Anneline Kriel, from South Africa.

NOVEMBER 29

Terrorist Meinhof Behind Bars

West German terrorist leader Ulrike Meinhof was today jailed for life for her part in the campaign of political assassinations and bombings carried out by the Red Army Faction, which aimed to bring down what it called 'the West German Fascist State'.

An intelligent woman with strong Christian beliefs, she had made an unlikely ringleader but, along with fellow conspirators Gudrun Ensslin and Andreas Baader - hence the gang's alternative name, 'the Baader-Meinhof Group' - had held Germany in a reign of terror before being arrested in 1972.

Meinhof would be found hanged in her cell in 1976, the other two dying in what was said to be a simultaneous suicide the following year.

Missing MP Stonehouse Found In Australia

BRITISH LABOUR MP JOHN STONEHOUSE, whose clothes were found on a Miami beach two months ago, and whose disappearance triggered an international hunt when police refused to believe he had committed suicide, reappeared in Australia today.

The former Postmaster-General, whose personal financial problems had led him to try to fake his own death, would fight attempts to extradite him to the UK to face charges of fraud, theft and deception, saying he wanted to start a new life in Australia.

Police investigations were centred on the dealings of a Bangladesh-based bank of which Stonehouse had been chairman before his disappearing-trick.

He would be unsuccessful in his fight against extradition, however, and was subsequently jailed following a much-publicized trial. He later wrote three thrillers, and was apparently a reformed character upon his release from prison. He died in 1988.

DECEMBER 25

Christmas Cyclone Devastates Darwin

There was no happy Christmas for the people of Queensland, Australia, today when the city of Darwin was laid waste by a cyclone, abruptly halting seasonal festivities and leaving a death-toll of nearly 50 in its wake.

Over half of the population was evacuated for safety reasons, while Prime Minister Gough Whitlam cut short a European trip to visit the scene, offer his condolences to victims, and promise a massive aid programme to local officials.

DECEMBER 10

Solzhenitsyn Collects Nobel Literature Prize

Russian author Alexander Isayevich Solzhenitsyn at last journeyed to Stockholm today to collect the Nobel Prize for Literature that he'd been awarded four years earlier, but had been refused permission to leave the Soviet Union to accept. A number of Eastern Bloc countries boycotted the ceremony in protest.

Solzhenitsyn thanked the Swedish Academy for making the award, which was largely for his two-volume exposé of Stalin's death-camps, *The Gulag Archipelago* - books which had made him famous in the West, but remained unpublished and banned in the country which expelled him in 1971.

In 1990, Solzhenitsyn would refuse a literary prize offered by the new post-communist Russian Republic for *The Gulag Archipelago,* saying he didn't wish to profit from the millions who had suffered in the Soviet labour camps. At that time, no official action had been taken to redress the wrongs of the past.

DECEMBER 21

Top London Store Bombed

Last-minute Christmas sales figures plummeted in London when shoppers were frightened away from the city centre by the IRA bomb which exploded in the top people's department store, Harrods, today.

It was the second such attack on a Central London shop to be carried out that week. Damage to the Knightsbridge store was extensive, although only one person sustained minor injuries. An emergency evacuation had been carried out following a telephone warning from an anonymous caller giving a recognized IRA identification code-name.

On December 22, IRA bombers hit the London home of Conservative Party leader Edward Heath. He was, fortunately, away at the time.

DECEMBER 7

Makarios Returns To Troubled Cyprus

AFTER A FIVE-MONTH EXILE in Malta and Britain following the attempted coup staged by Greek nationalist army officers, and the Turkish invasion of Cyprus, Archbishop Makarios returned to the troubled Mediterranean island for the first time today.

A staunch supporter of political union with Greece, the Greek Cypriot shepherd's son who became President had survived several other assassination attempts earlier in the year - something which had dogged his political life since the late 1950s, when his alleged involvement with the outlawed EOKA terrorist organization had led to his arrest by the governing British authorities and deportation into a two-year exile in the Seychelles and mainland Greece.

Although he had beaten off physical and political attacks from Greek and Turkish extremists in the intervening years, he had been powerless to prevent the division of Cyprus which followed the Turkish invasion, although he did recognize the Turkish right to self-government.

Swing-Wing White Elephant

The US Air Force's B-1 *swing-wing* bomber made its first successful test-flight this month, to begin what would prove a controversial career. The massive aircraft with its variable-geometry 'swing-wing' technology could carry twice the bomb-load of the B-52 *Stratofortress* , the mainstay of US strategic bombing capability since World War II. It was intended to form the third and most flexible component of the so-called 'triad' defence system alongside land-based and submarine-launched ballistic missiles.

The B-1 programme would be cancelled in 1977 by President Carter, who favoured the cheaper, unmanned cruise missile, but was resurrected by President Ronald Reagan to enter service as an expensive and - after the end of the cold war - unnecessary white elephant.

Carter's Bid For White House

In Atlanta today, Jimmy Carter, the 50-year-old head of his family's peanut-farming business and Governor of Georgia for the previous eight years, declared his intention to run for the Democratic Party's presidential nomination in 1975. Born in Plains, Georgia, where he still had his family home and business, Carter had attended the US Naval Academy and served in the US Navy as a nuclear engineer until 1953. Entering politics in the early 1960s, he spent his early career as a senator before winning his present post for the first time.

Healey Faces Inflation Explosion

It's unlikely that Britain's Chancellor of the Exchequer, Denis Healey, had much time to devote to celebrating over Christmas, or that he looked forward to 1975 with much hope. Despite what his supporters had described as a positive budget in November, the country was faced with galloping inflation.

A spiral of price and wage increases had pushed up the cost of living in 1974 by 20 per cent in September, with British industry crippled by higher pay demands and rapidly rising prices of raw materials. December's official figures showed inflation at 26 per cent.

Mr Healey's November budget had boosted that inflation rate by dropping price controls for nationalized industries and slapping a high tax on petrol prices. While a gallon of 4-star petrol had cost the British motorist 42p ($1.10) in January, it looked as if the cost would be closer to 80p ($2.10) a year later!

Unlike most Western horoscope systems which group astrological signs into month-long periods based on the influence of 12 constellations, the Chinese believe that those born in the same year of their calendar share common qualities with one of 12 animals - Rat, Ox, Tiger, Rabbit, Dragon, Snake, Horse, Sheep, Monkey, Rooster, Dog or Pig.

They also allocate the general attributes of five natural elements - Earth, Fire, Metal, Water, Wood - and an overall positive or negative aspect to each sign to summarize its qualities.

If you were born between February 29, 1973 and January 22, 1974, you are an Ox. As this book is devoted to the events of 1974, let's take a look at the sign which governs those born between January 23 that year and February 10, 1975 - The Year of The Tige

THE TIGER
JANUARY 23, 1974 - FEBRUARY 10, 1975
ELEMENT: METAL   ASPECT: (+)

Tigers are born leaders. They like to be in charge and the centre of attention. This comes from an innate ability to take command of any situation and run the show.

Tigers often bend the rules to suit themselves. They enjoy taking risks and have the confidence to achieve anything they want. They challenge the world alone and don't succumb to what others might think or say. They get whatever they might want or need as they have no fear of asking, learning by experience and observation.

They are not the type to take advice too kindly, should they ever need to, but this doesn't mean they're arrogant or self-promoting. On the contrary, Tigers have an inherent magnetic personality. They are friendly, talkative and interested in everyone and everything. They will always give good, honest, frank advice and possess a wide-eyed cunning innocence which is very approachable.

Tigers are compassionate, with a humanitarian approach to life and worldly problems. They will not let injustice pass by unnoticed and insist on voicing their own opinions, often leading by maybe taking the law into their own hands. The Tiger thrives on challenge.

Being adventurers gives Tigers an immense amount of energy. They can sweep everyone and everything along in their enthusiam. They are unpredictable and live for the moment, which makes them exciting.

Tigers do have their faults. They can be bad-tempered, impatient, aggressive and defensive. This comes from their unwavering conviction that what they believe is right. They are always eager to carry through their intentions and ideals, however rebellious and non-conforming they may be.

Tigers enjoy life and, as leaders, ensure their followers appreciate it as much. They are generous with all they've learned and earned, and will always ensure a global solution rather than personal gain to any problem or query.

FAMOUS TIGERS

Her Majesty the Queen
David Attenborough
Conservationist, TV wildlife guru
Richard Branson
Founder/chairman of The Virgin Group
Valéry Giscard D'Estaing
French statesman, former President of France
Sir Alec Guinness

Stage and film actor
David Owen
British politician,diplomat
Rudolf Nureyev
Russian born ballet superstar
Dame Diana Rigg
Stage and film actress
Stevie Wonder
Singer, songwriter, multi-instrumentalist, producer